GET STARTED
AS A
FILM EXTRA

- UK Edition -

P.R.WALTON

P.R.WALTON

INTRODUCTION

The idea for this book came about when I realised how many fresh faces were joining the industry with questions and a desire for stories and guidance from seasoned film extras. I have spent more than a decade in this fascinating industry since my first job back in 2010 and it's been a crazy ride ever since. Some good, some bad. Why not share that with the world?

For the most part, this is a guide with the purpose of sharing information and useful knowledge. But it can also provide an inside look at the film industry with snippets of my own experiences. I tried to keep it structured as I cover as many topics as possible, and hopefully this writing will inspire, encourage and teach.

Notes: Some facts and figures may change over time as this book was written at the start of 2024 and the industry evolves at a fast pace. Great care has been taken not to break any non-disclosure agreements. All experiences are personal to me, and opinions and events may differ from person to person.

CONTENTS

1 THE ROLE

Film Extras have been necessary on screen since the very early days of filmmaking when productions would find people from local communities to make up the numbers needed for scenes. During the Golden Age of Hollywood (between the 1920s and 1950s), agencies would handle castings for the roles, and the emergence of unions such as SAG and Equity began improving wages and working conditions. As decades passed, television opened further opportunities, castings became more efficient, and roles included a lot more diversity.

"Film Extra" is the most recognisable term for industry outsiders, but there are other name variations used when talking about this profession:

- Background Actor

- Background Artist
- Supporting Artist
- Extra
- Crowd

I call myself a *Film Extra* when talking to friends and family because that's easy for them to understand. Everyone knows what that means. But the term you will hear most often on set nowadays would be **Supporting Artist** (abbreviated to *SA*) or **Crowd.** The United States has even more names to add to the list and have been known to do things a little different to us over here in the UK. I would love to read a US version to see all the comparisons and similarities. But that's why I've made this book a UK edition; I can write from personal understanding and experience and there won't be any confusion or mix-ups.

All kinds of people make up the pool of SA's - retirees, students, freelancers, business owners, those with spare time around other commitments, and occasionally you meet individuals who have made this a full-time profession. I have made a living from this industry for the last two years, but I'm earning well below the national average, and I won't lie, I carry around anxiety over my finances and whether I'll be able to cover all my monthly bills. Some people travel up and down the country making good money from the work. A lifestyle I admire but could never do myself. I prefer to stick to areas I'm familiar with - London and the South East.

There are no wrong appearances in this line of work. You can be taller than average, shorter, thicker, thinner, older, younger… Everyone has a chance of finding a role. I'll be honest and say that some looks get more work than others due to being versatile enough to fit a variety of genres, time periods and character types, but nobody will be excluded from SA work due to the way they look, stylise, identify etc. This is an industry that welcomes all.

Most people look to start being a film extra on a part-time basis to fit it around a day job, and others may only want to do the job once or twice to check off a bucket list item. When I first started, I was in a full-time job and worked on average three days a year in SA work. After many years, I left my job to go to university and then worked on film sets during Easter and Summer holidays. After graduating, I had more confidence that I could survive in the industry, and I took the risk to stay self-employed as an extra instead of finding another career or day job. This was a gradual process and I believe that it would be near impossible to jump straight into this full-time without proving yourself to agencies for being reliable and professional first.

So, what do SA's do?

The job of an SA is not to be a star. We are on set to work quietly in the background while professional actors do the heavier workload. We *are* important though. Scenes come alive with the addition of Supporting Artists. We prevent them from feeling flat and add ambience and realism. We could be part of exposition shots which set the scene, feature in the foreground for a point of view shot, or simply create hustle and activity behind the main cast for movement and depth. Some productions may show you in great detail, while others will leave you wondering if the blurred arm that crossed in front of the camera was you. There could be times where your scene (or in my case, an entire TV show) is cut and never sees the light of day.

One time, I was convinced I would be clearly visible on a popular HBO show after spending a week working on it at Leavesden Studios outside London (now known as Warner Bros. Studios). Multiple cameras were set up on the crowd, and some of the activity going on in the script indicated that our reactions would be very important. When the show aired, I could not find a single frame where I was visible. My ego was bruised for all of three seconds before I continued enjoying the episode. Whereas, on an episode of a well-loved Netflix show, I appeared in nearly every frame of a scene which took me by surprise… in clear detail! This was the first real evidence my friends and family had that I actually work in the film and television industry and can earn money from it. Thankfully since seeing this, my family no longer announces to me every job vacancy that crops up in our local town. They used to think I was a cash-strapped creative with no direction in life. It was a correct assumption to have.

As for the TV show I mentioned that never saw the light of day… That kept me going for a whole Summer, with money flowing regularly into my bank account and to my savings. It seemed like it was going to be a good show until the network decided it wasn't worth airing. I believe it can be sold off to be aired by another network or streaming platform, so there's still a small chance it will rear its head.

By using paid SA's instead of real people (i.e. general members of the public), productions have full control and can make sure costumes are appropriately styled and reset everyone for each take to keep continuity. When cameras shoot multiple angles, it's important that movements and timings are the same so that the final edit looks seamless. Audiences can find the viewing experience jarring to watch otherwise. Even "reality" tv shows use extras to maintain control, continuity and professionalism while shooting. I won't name any names for fear of being targeted by unhappy Producers, but I think you may already know some examples. In my early days of this profession, I worked on one, pretending to be a member of the public in a restaurant and I was allowed to drag a family member along for the excitement. We got a free meal out of it which we were told to eat very slowly, but neither of us were paid. Free work is something I would never do nowadays, and it shouldn't be necessary for newbies. I was just un-informed and naive at the time.

If you successfully make it as a film extra, you may encounter the following questions from friends and family who are intrigued and curious about your strange-yet-fabulous lifestyle choices:

"Do you not want a real job?"
"So, what have I seen you in?"
"Met anyone famous?"

"How do you get into that, then?"
"Have you been on Eastenders?"
"Aren't Hollywood films shot in America?"
"You must be making a ton of money now, right?"
"Could you get me Margot Robbie's autograph?"
"Why do you never show me photos of you on the set?"
"Aren't you bored of this hobby?"

Sadly, I have become accustomed to either being vague, or telling white lies in response to what I've worked on because I'm terrified of landing myself in hot water. Especially before it's released or announced. One of my siblings wouldn't think twice about blabbing to a British tabloid that *Doctor Who* had been secretly filming under the codename [redacted information] in the location of [redacted information] and they heard it directly from a trustworthy source. So, I lie. *"Oh, last week? Yeah, I was busy working on some period show no one's heard of. Yawn."* It may or may not have been *Game of Thrones*.

I have a whole chapter dedicated to this topic of secrecy later on in the book. It's a big deal with some companies taking it more seriously than others. (Looking at you, Disney!)

Here are some of my own answers in case any readers also had these questions on their mind:-

Yes, sometimes I consider quitting and getting a real job. You may have seen a blurred glimpse of me on stuff for Marvel, Disney, Netflix, BBC, ITV, Amazon Prime, Sky, many commercials, and even a video game! Yes, I've met and spoken with famous people like George Clooney, Olivia Colman, Evangeline Lilly, Julianne Moore and Michelle Pfeiffer. I got into this work through simply googling "how to get into films" and signing up to a recommended agency. Yes, I've been on Eastenders… twice! And it was amazing! Hollywood films come to shoot in the UK a lot for reasons I explain in the next chapter. I can make good money per day, though it's hard to fill the calendar with lots of work. No autographs or selfies with the cast, unfortunately. There are strict rules that prevent photography on set unless it's authorised by the Production Office for professional behind-the-scenes or stills. I will never get bored of this job.

And what if a person wants to become more than an Extra?

My family get confused about my job and often quiz me with questions like *"why don't you ever get lines to say?"* And I have to explain over and over that *acting* agencies are required for that type of thing, as well as time and money spent on training and auditions. Becoming an actor is not easy, and I am currently dabbling with crossing over into that after completing a lengthy training course, but I know there's a lot of hard work required and a generous helping of luck needed to make a success of it. The luck part will annoy some people… I truly believe this can play a big part.

A point to add for those who have an interest in going beyond extra work to become an actor: If you're a startup actor hoping to get showreel material, this is not the reliable way to achieve that. You want to instead focus on student films or independent productions where there is a better chance of screen time and dialogue.

Sadly, Casting Directors don't care much for those who openly discuss their history of being SA's. I've met people very serious about their acting craft who say that they can't announce they were once seen running across a set on a massive-budget Marvel film as buildings fell around them, because drama schools had taught them it could affect chances to be taken seriously as an actor. When listed with current famous people who had once been SA's, they shrug and furiously scrub all traces of their participation from online platforms and social media. My arguments go unheard as I plead to anyone who will listen to my moaning about how being an SA teaches us to work professionally around high profile individuals, to memorise cues and hit marks, the logistics of a film set, the roles of each department, and makes one appreciate how a good breakfast and strong coffee can keep the momentum of the day going. I will forever hold the belief that our job provides valuable learning experiences for those who eventually want to step up and get into professional screen acting, or careers in a crew department.

2 TYPES OF WORK

Some of the project-types we work on can include **feature films, independent films, TV shows, pilots, commercials, music videos, games, corporate videos, and stills.** And not just British ones either; There are numerous productions that come over from the US with reasons ranging from the diverse locations available in our country and our quality studio spaces, to the financial benefits of tax breaks and strong investments. I also hear we have some of the best editors over here? Unsure how true that statement is. Hollywood brings in great revenue for the UK and plenty of job opportunities.

There is also a large Bollywood presence over here from India that does a lot of work across the country. However, this is met with some controversy. Many people have reported good experiences on Bollywood productions, with friendly crew, ample amounts of work, and great food… whilst others have reported that production companies have disappeared without paying people for all the work done. I have never done Bollywood myself but would be open to considering it. If I do find myself with this opportunity, I would certainly approach with caution and research how reliable the Bollywood-focused agencies are and whether the production has a good record of paying out before committing. A way of doing this is to reach out to other Supporting Artists on the many existing Facebook or WhatsApp groups and ask for their experiences.

Oddly enough, I've been in more Hollywood films than I have British TV dramas. I think that's to do with my location. Many TV dramas are based further North of the country, whereas Hollywood typically stays in the South to use the larger studios located around the M25 *(Pinewood, Warner Bros, Longcross, Shepperton, Sky Studios Elstree etc)*, and London is a popular backdrop for action sequences. Americans don't care as much to see villains being chased around Sheffield or Leeds.

Types of SA's

The typical job will require you to be a generic supporting artist used to populate the scene. But there are other types of SA roles that you can be booked under. You can be **featured** on screen, have **dialogue** to say, perform a specialist **skill** (like playing a musical instrument, dancing, ice skating etc), **standing in** for cast during technical setups for camera and lighting, **doubling** for cast (not to be confused with stunt doubling), or performing as a **SPACT** artist (Special Action - meaning to perform action skills that don't necessarily require highly trained stunt performers.

One example is being part of a large crowd of sword fighters to fill the background behind the cast or stunts team). These types of jobs are a little harder to get, but once you've proven yourself a few times, you can find the frequency of these requests increasing. And you will earn more money doing a day as one of these "upgrades", in comparison to the typical Supporting Artist.

So far, I have been a stand-in and picture double. Standing in required my full focus to understand the actor's movements and timings in order to do my job well when they stepped off-set, and I replaced them. I found this to be more of an extension of the crew really. I wasn't there to perform. I was there to work with the camera team as a useful pawn so they could figure out the logistics of the shot. Doubling felt like more of an acting role. I was given my own dressing room in one of the trailers, and I was prepared by the same costume and hair & makeup team that usually worked with the main cast. On set, I followed strict instructions, precisely matching movements to create a shot that can blend seamlessly within a scene shot by the actual actor. The job here is to disguise myself as someone else who perhaps was unavailable, lacked the necessary skill or physique, or didn't feel comfortable performing a piece of the scene. A lot of effort went into this - a wig, makeup, costume alterations, even a manicure.

The agencies don't usually pass on information like how many other SA's you'll be working with. Sometimes you rock up and realise very quickly you are just a number in the hundreds of people hired for the day. Or you could experience the opposite and be one of few working that day.

I once turned up to a job confused by the lack of cars in the carpark thinking I had turned up on the wrong day, to discover that I was the only supporting artist booked in. That piled on a lot of pressure, but it was a super relaxed day. I was in a makeshift hospital bed, as the main actor does a scene in the bed beside me with a nurse. Easy. You do develop a bit of paranoia, however. Am I lying down weirdly? Is my posture bad? Am I being too still? Should I fidget more to look alive? Regardless, the director must have been happy with my background performance because she never said a word to me. I was wrapped after 45 minutes on set, and I toddled off past the actor and crew who thanked me for my hard work. The awkwardness of this alone made me deserving of the £100 I had earned that day. This was a bit of a tangent from the chapter's topic, but I'm trying to include as many on-set stories as possible to make this book interesting. So, here's another for you…

On the opposite end of the spectrum, I arrived at a job many years ago for a feature film and walked into the largest marquee I had even seen, lined with tables and chairs. This was a job with around 500 extras and a big Crowd team to manage it all. We had all been told our numbers at the costume fittings a month earlier and it was also scribbled down on scrap pieces of paper and handed to us as we signed in for the first morning. Over the ten days working on this, instead of hearing names or groups like "upper class characters" or "men only", we would have numbers yelled at us. "Numbers 001 to 125 to travel to set!" If it wasn't numbers being called, it was, "People who were in that shot with the drone, put your lunch down and head back to set!" As chaotic as it sounds, I remember it running smoothly with very few mix-ups. And although it was a tiring job with early starts and late finishes, it was the first job where I had the blues after we wrapped, and I longed to return.

Apparently, actors also get the blues after working on films, and it may be the same for many SA's and Crew who have been part of one project for a while. It seems to occur when you've adapted to the film-set routine and are seeing the same faces each day, getting looked after continuously, and it can be quite a transition leaving that world behind to go back to normal life.

3 JOINING AN AGENCY

(You'll be pleased to know that this chapter contains a
handy little list of good agencies!)

There are many agencies across the UK to sign up with.
Unlike acting or modelling agencies, no SA agency should
make you sign up exclusively to them. I did hear of one
further up north of the country trying to prevent people on
their books from signing up to anyone else. That's an
immediate red flag.

There are (typically) two types of agencies. **Commission**
only, and **subscription** based. Many people warn to stay
away from agencies who ask for upfront money as a signup fee or ongoing subscription, which is typically correct.
However, there can be exceptions to this. *Universal Extras*
and *Talent Talks* are two agencies that can provide good
opportunities in the industry, and both require an upfront
subscription to be considered for their full range of jobs.
They are the only two pay-upfront platforms I would ever
consider. They get some brilliant opportunities in, but you
need to consider the risk of whether you will actually get

jobs through them. Some SA's say these are their best agencies, others will say they paid the upfront fee but never got selected for any jobs. I've been with both of these platforms and find them hit or miss. There are options to be with them both for free as well, but this limits your chances.

My first experience with *Universal Extras* was poor. I signed up for a three-year membership and only had three days of work in that time. When that membership lapsed, I left them alone for a good number of years. After becoming more experienced, I thought I would try them out again. I registered for another three years. In that time, I had about twenty-five days of work, and one of them was the best job I have worked to date. I was offered a role as a picture double for the lead actor on a very popular Netflix series. Great money, great experience, and one of the hardest secrets I ever had to keep until its release date. Despite this, I still feel like this agency is very low on my list of recommendations. *Universal Extras* are high maintenance and very fussy about photos. I've had pictures rejected because they thought I messed with the saturation (I hadn't), because the background wasn't white enough, because they can see the very edge of a light switch, because there's too much headroom, and the list goes on. Other SA's who have been in this profession for years, even decades have trouble getting photos approved. Then there's the issue where they automatically pencil all your available dates on a job request 'just in case' the production needs you. Very poor practice. I also find myself not being told much about the jobs, whereas people on set who had booked their work through a different agency will rock up knowing whether the parking fees are being reimbursed, what time the estimate wrap is, whether the day is **standard** (where you get an hour lunch break) or **continuous** (where there isn't a dedicated lunch break and you eat on-the-go), and what your expected earnings for the day might look like. I can't even get a response from this agency about those queries. But as I said, despite their flaws they do provide decent opportunities.

Talent Talks are similar in that you pay upfront to apply for the jobs on their website. They occasionally post open castings so it's worth keeping an eye out on their jobs board even if you aren't a full member. This agency deals mostly in commercials and music videos, but I've had some feature films through them, and have seen them casting hundreds of people for a famous Disney franchise. I initially had a one-year membership many years ago and had numerous days on a job. But then the work dried up, so I didn't continue. I tried again more recently and had better success. A lot of their stuff are one-day gigs that I can fit around other things, making it great to fill the time, but opportunities are slowing down again for me on there. I think people with more modern appearances will have better success. I keep my appearance rather boring to get period work, and that's probably too bland for their clients. Reviews from other SA's are mixed with some not getting work from them, and others doing great and receiving well-paid roles with features and buyouts. I'll probably continue to stay with them for the near future.

The more standard agencies are the best in my opinion. They are easy to navigate and low maintenance. They earn their money through **commission**, and some will also take a **book fee** from your first job of the period (a period can be twelve to eighteen months before it renews). I'm not sure why book fees still exist when everything is done digitally nowadays, but for some reason this practice continues to be normal and doesn't show signs of vanishing any time soon. It can come as a shock when you do a day's work, and the deductions leave you with pennies. The lowest I've been paid after a job is £9.14 and that was after being on a BBC series where I had the commission and book fee deducted from my total earnings. Luckily the job was local, so I wasn't exactly out of pocket.

The pool of SA's is consistently growing making it a highly saturated market. Some agencies will be very difficult to sign up with because they don't want too many on their database. A good example of this is *Ray Knight Casting* who are notoriously difficult to sign with. I tried for six years, then struck lucky when they were in need of more natural looking people for period dramas. Then there's another where I've been on their waitlist for six years. If it proves difficult to find agencies with open books, check back regularly on their website or social media for *urgent castings* until something comes along that you're suited to, and keep all your applications up to date, so that as soon as they need more people like you, your profile will be ready.

Here is a list of some of the reputable agencies and platforms in the industry which will be useful:-

- CASTING COLLECTIVE
- EXTRA PEOPLE
- RAY KNIGHT CASTING

- RACHEL'S PEOPLE
- ENTERTAINMENT PARTNERS
- SLICK CASTING
- ONSET EXTRAS
- PIECE OF CAKE CASTING
- PHOENIX CASTING
- NORF CASTING
- CELEX CASTING
- BETTY'S & DUDES
- CREATIVE CASTING
- * TALENT TALKS
- * UNIVERSAL EXTRAS

Requires a signup fee and has a jobs board where the artist submits themselves for work. Research and read reviews first before committing. I believe Universal Extras is free for students.

There is another big agency left off the list, but at time of writing, they are showing signs of financial difficulty with artists not being paid for work they did over six months ago, so I refuse to mention them in this book. I don't think they will be around much longer anyway due to the negative publicity they've recently had and the collapse of trust in them.

I am with eight of the agencies on the above list. And the others cover geographical areas outside of my area - across Wales, North of England, Scotland. There isn't much point in me applying for those because I will only travel a maximum of 90 minutes for a job, preferably under an hour. But I've known of artists who will travel all over the place staying in a converted van or camper and they manage to stay relatively busy with consistent work each week.

The **Entertainment Partners** platform (used to be known as *POP* before being acquired in 2020) essentially works as a database that stores your profile and allows smaller agencies to approach you with availability requests for jobs. So, once you've signed up to this platform, you can find emails landing in your inbox from *Sabell Casting, Camera Action Extras, Two 10 Casting, Key Casting, Lucas Extras* and many others! This is one worth signing up to. The only negative point is that the commissions are higher because 10% of your earnings plus VAT goes to the platform, and then an additional 10% plus VAT goes to the agency. Other agencies not on the platform typically take around 15% plus the VAT.

There are lots of scams out there trying to take advantage of those trying to break into the industry. There is no requirement for professional photographs or "portfolios", and it's best to play it safe by not paying signup fees until you've developed knowledge or gained experience and advice from other SA's who can safely recommend them. Even though I gave recommendations above of pay-to-join platforms, gather more information on them first and make sure you're the right fit before blindly handing them your money. *Talent Talks*, for example, is better suited to the younger, contemporary demographic.

Another story time: when I was relatively new to all this, I contacted an agency who did extra work and modelling to join their database. They invited me in for a chat and to take some photographs to put onto my profile. I went, had the photos taken, and all was good. Afterwards they showed me some of the photos which looked great, then they said that nobody would see my profile or hire me until I paid the agency £500 for a portfolio to be put on their database. I said I had to think about it. They replied that I needed to hurry because there was a big client wanting to book lots of artists and that I'd be perfect. I left and blocked them. A few years later, it surfaced that hundreds of people had been pressured into paying this hefty fee and never heard from the 'agency' ever again. This is a common scam that people face on a regular basis when trying to break into the industry.

4 THE PERFECT PROFILE

A good profile will be filled out with as much information as possible, including precise **measurements**, your list of **skills**, and any **uniforms** or specialist clothing you own. You'll be prompted to upload your **National Insurance Number**, a **DBS certificate** that has been issued in the last 18 months, a form of **ID** (passport, birth certificate, driving licence), and **bank details** to receive payments. Agency platforms are good at guiding you through the process of setting up a good profile, but it's up to the artist to keep everything up-to-date and accurate.

A note about applying for a DBS certificate - make sure you use official government sites to apply. There are third-party sites that rip people off with higher charges. These are the official web addresses to apply for yours, depending on where you're located:-

England: https://www.gov.uk/request-copy-criminal-record

Northern Ireland:
https://www.nidirect.gov.uk/campaigns/accessni-criminal-record-checks

Scotland: https://www.mygov.scot/basic-disclosure/apply-for-basic-disclosure

The cost at the moment is £18 for England and Northern Ireland, or £25 for Scotland. This may change in the future. You're expected to apply every 18 months for a new basic check. This cost can be deducted as expenses which I'll discuss later in the *Finances* chapter.

Most, or all profiles will have some sort of calendar to view which lists the work you are booked for, pencilled for or have answered available to. This is useful if you've lost track and to help avoid clashes. And you can block out dates that you are unavailable for. I find it easier to track them on my phone calendar instead of logging in to different platforms all the time. However, it can be good using the agency platforms to see if you've been released as sometimes you mistakenly aren't notified.

Photos

There's no need to purchase professional photographs, especially with the quality most phones can produce. Most of my profile photos are taken on my phone and have earned me many gigs. Some people invest in a ring light which is also useful for taking pictures and recording self-tapes, and I have a function on my phone where I can set a timer of up to 10 seconds to allow me to get into position before it automatically captures the image. You may get the odd agency that want to take your photos for you so that their database looks uniformed. As long as they don't charge a fee then this is okay. If you turn up for a quick photoshoot, and they start pressuring you to pay money to get your profile up and running, immediately walk away! This is either a scam, or a shady way to make some quick cash. *Ray Knight Casting* is an example of a trustworthy agency that prefers to take their own photos of you, and it will be for free!

My advice on photos is:

- To have approximately 4-6 photos on each profile
- Show variety - hair up/down, head and shoulders, full body
- Update the selfies section every 5-6 weeks showing a neutral expression and natural hair texture (head and shoulders, side profile, and back of head)
- Use good natural lighting from a window and plain backgrounds where possible
- Don't edit the photos!!! There is no need to blur skin texture, whiten teeth, or cover grey hairs. Those imperfections are actually more likely to get you work

I've seen posts of frustration from newcomers wondering why they weren't selected for the last couple seasons of *The Crown*, all the while refusing to upload photos without their vertically laminated eyebrows, or contoured makeup and thick coats of mascara. Their photos are edited to look like advertising campaigns, and their mentality is *the prettier I am, the more film and television producers will want me*. Nothing could be further from the truth. **The more you can blend in, the more work you can potentially get.**

As I said earlier, you can find some good guidance and tips on agency websites during the application process. Some are more high maintenance about what they want than others. For example, do you remember my examples of *Universal Extras* rejecting photos for the oddest reasons? *Casting Collective* are a little more relaxed about what you upload, as long as it's a clear and current representation of you.

The selfie section probably sounds weird to newcomers. It's expected that these are updated on a more frequent basis than your standard profile photos. Departments such as Assistant Director's (AD's), Hair & Makeup (HMU/MU), and Costume find these photos useful to see your current look and ensure you are a right fit for the character you're being asked to play. They don't care how photogenic you are. They care whether they can envision you blending into the scene in character. The makeup team can also plan whether they need to style some wigs or prepare to cover any visible tattoos. They'd rather not have to do these extra steps as they have a limit on how long they can spend getting individuals ready on the morning of a shoot. So, it may be that one small tattoo on your collarbone can prevent you from getting period work, unless a large crowd is required, and they are struggling to find suitable people.

That's when they'll be willing to take those extra steps for a few SA's to make up the numbers required for filming.

5 CASTING PROCESS

A production will contact an agency with a brief they need fulfilling. *Twenty-five French-looking men in their thirties to play soldiers, must have SPACT experience and be physically fit.* The agency will go through their database and check the availability of those who fit the brief by email/text/phone call. If the artist says they are available, they will be forwarded to production who will make selections.

Usually, plenty of people will be put forward to the production with only a handful being selected. This part of the process can be disappointing for many who feel like despite all the AV's, they don't seem to be booking in the work. I've heard stories of people who have a medical career outside of SA work turned down to play doctors and nurses in favour of those inexperienced in the medical profession who 'looked more like the part'. It can be frustrating, but we suck it up and move on. Or we think about it bitterly. *How do I not qualify as a generic passerby when I do that daily?*

There are various ways a production chooses their SA's… it can be first-come-first-serve, a random selection, those who fit the look best, input from other departments, or faces that are recognised from previous jobs. I was booked immediately on a particular show because the AD team had been on a previous show with me and I'd proven to be professional, easy to work with and reliable. Plus, the time period was similar, and I suited the look well. It essentially became a small reunion which was nice. Then there was another job where everyone's names started with the letters A-G, and it became obvious they went down an alphabetically sorted list selecting each person until they had the correct number of individuals.

Occasionally you could be asked to provide a self-tape, or in rare circumstances, attend an audition if the role is featured, involves dialogue, or requires a specific skill. I've had to do a few self-tapes in my time, and once attended an audition at a studio for swordfighters on a production along with hundreds of other people. It was brilliant fun, but I sadly didn't get the role.

Keeping expectations realistic avoids disappointment - whether that's to do with the amount of work you think you'll get, the productions you've dreamed of working on (I'm ignoring my own advice and still waiting in hope for the new Harry Potter series with my fingers crossed for getting some work on it!), ideas of becoming famous, or the expectation that you'll be seen in the final edit… After working hundreds of days as a Supporting Artist, I've only been properly seen five times on screen. The rest of the time I've been an unrecognisable blur, or a distant figure in a sea of   faces.

6 CHARACTERS

You will be cast depending on your suitability to the character needed. For a scene set in a school, 16–24-year-olds with a young look are more likely to be cast as pupils/students to populate the school, with a sprinkling of 30+ year olds playing teachers. Having real children on set brings limitations such as restricted working hours and further costs for the hiring of chaperones. So, while there may be some under sixteen-year-olds on set, you can usually spot many adults playing kids. Examples include *Grease (1978)*, *St. Trinians (2007)*, and BBC's *Waterloo Road*.

Castings can also be about your physical look with build, hair, height, tattoos etc taken into account. I don't often work on modern day projects because I don't look contemporary enough. I don't have quirky hair or decent fashionable taste. I intentionally keep my appearance bland and unkempt as it gives me great roles in period dramas. Someone with facial piercings and a head of highlights wouldn't be put forward for consideration on things like *Bridgerton* or *Call The Midwife* but they may have good success in music videos and commercials. Men have particular struggles with the length of their hair and how much facial hair they should have. Different time periods need different lengths and styles, and it can be hard adapting to each production when many projects overlap with each other. I'm desperate to chop all my hair off, but I'm currently on a long-running production, and as I approach the end of my time with them, I will soon start on another long-running production… The best I can do is get a trim and wait until later in the year when I'm no longer on productions with lots of days before I go for the big cut.

The range of time periods a person may cover is huge. I have been in almost every time period from Medieval to Dystopian. The Victorian era is my most visited, but my favourite to dress up in is the 70s/80s/90s - comfier footwear, less pins or wigs in the hair, and it's easy to dress yourself without requiring a team around you. I also just love the look of these decades.

It seems I have been typecast as the lower class or peasant characters, which to be honest is great! In the rare times I've had to play someone upper class, the costumes have been a lot more uncomfortable, and you get fussed over by the costume and makeup departments more. I'm also typically cast as a businessperson for modern day settings, or occasionally a police officer. The strangest two days was when I worked on a show as a peasant covered in dirt, then the following day I was on a commercial with a well-known

American actor, splashing around at a fancy pool party. The juxtaposition was odd.

These are some examples of the kind of on-screen **characters** a supporting artist may be asked to play:

- Passerby
- Waiter/Waitress
- Cafe Customer
- Townsfolk
- Dancer
- Musician
- Police Officer
- Party Guest
- Concertgoer
- Security
- Journalist
- Paparazzi
- Elf
- Student
- Commuter
- Office Worker
- Escort
- Receptionist
- Villager
- Clubber
- Protestor
- Doctor/Nurse

- Passenger
- Funeral Mourner
- Shopkeeper
- Hospital Patient
- Tourist
- Soldier
- Parent
- Deceased Body
- Prisoner
- Film Crew
- Swimmer
- Sports Fan
- Servant
- Wedding Guest
- Peasant
- CIA Agent
- Alien
- Fighter

I have in fact, been 95% of these characters over the years! The most difficult one for me has been clubber; if a scene requires two main characters having a conversation in a loud club with music, the crowd of SA's are usually working silently… There is no music playing for a majority of takes, the props department would have told everyone to *pretend* to sip their drinks so they don't have to keep topping up, and all that background talking/singing/laughing will be mimed. I hate miming. I also hate dancing. It is not a good mix for me. But I'll still say yes to those jobs though, for money's sake.

There are times where the scene requires tens of thousands of people for the background, but the budget can only accommodate 200 extras (this is an example scenario). In these circumstances, the VFX team will scan selected people to create 3D-image characters, or film them on a blue screen (as a group or individually). The results are composited into scenes to make crowds look bigger. On FAA/PACT rate jobs, there is an additional supplementary payment of approximately £28.83 (as of 2024) added to your payment, although I recommend you check that your image is only being used for that same production and that it doesn't put you at risk of losing out on future work. I'm not sure it's as big a problem in the UK but definitely seems to be a growing issue in the US.

7 COSTUME FITTINGS

Fittings are required when productions purchase or hire costumes to supply to the artist. You are typically called to a costume fitting in advance of the shoot day for uniformed characters such as police officers or for older time periods like the Victorian-era.

The fitting experience tends to be consistent across most jobs and should only take a few hours, except in the case of more intricate clothing selections. I had one fitting that went over the four-hour mark which immediately increased my pay to a full day rate instead of the half day I was originally going to receive. Most of those hours were spent sat patiently in a waiting room until the costume team were available. They struggled to find an outfit that fit me well enough, then the makeup artist took her time putting tight curls into my hair. You get see the AD was stressed about this. I suspect they are under pressure to keep costs down and avoid things like this happening. It was a huge budget movie though, so I don't feel too guilty.

Call details are sent beforehand and will contain the calltime, location, emergency contact number, and whether you have to bring anything specific with you such as accessories, tights or outfit options. This location could be at a studio, in an empty building the council have been trying to sell, in old offices, inside a trailer at the unit base of wherever the production is at that time, at a warehouse, or in a marquee on some farmland. I've been to all these places for various fittings across London and the South East.

An AD will be there to sign you in and direct you to different departments. There's usually a bit of waiting at the start until the Costume dept. are ready for you, then you're taken through to get measured and try on options. The most important part here is to make sure you'll be comfortable spending a whole day/week/month in the outfit. I once made the mistake of putting up with an uncomfortably tight jacket because it looked good, and it would only be for a day. They asked me to return for multiple more days after that shoot day and it was hell. If any part of your outfit, such as the shoes, are uncomfortable, this is the best time to say, as there may be no spare ones to swap to during the shoot. Once they have settled on the right costume for you, they may consider accessories such as hats, jewellery, and bags before sending you back to the AD.

You will then be escorted to Makeup, if necessary, still dressed in the outfit. Here, they will decide what hairstyle to give you, whether you need wigs or prosthetics, and check for any tattoos that need covering. Then they'll take pictures of your head & shoulders from straight on, both side profiles, and from the back.

You will be asked to return to Costume again where you have full-body photos taken. Finally, they let you change back into your own clothes, before releasing you to go back to Makeup where any pins & pieces can be returned, or makeup/prosthetics removed. The AD will sign you out and you are done for the day.

Costume fittings are a good opportunity to find out more about the shoot, as up until now, you would have been provided with very limited information. I find it useful to ask if the shoot is interior or exterior, whether it's a film or a show, maybe some of the story, or how many other SA's will be in the same scenes. More often than not, crew are happy to share a snippet of information at fittings. The question I always have on hand is "what season of the year is this set in?" Say your filming days are scheduled during an icy blast in February, but the scene is supposed to be set in late Summer, you will need to take this opportunity to evaluate your costume and think about how many layers of thermals and thick socks you can hide beneath the outfit so that you stay warm enough. For some bizarre reason, *which totally makes sense when it's explained properly*, it's normal to be shooting opposite seasons. During Winter I've had to wear Spring/Summer costumes with short sleeves, and in

Summer I've been horrendously wrapped up in woollen outfits. Only once have I seen a person faint!

A lot of the time, crowd fittings are done in a separate location to the cast. But I've had a few times where they've been at the same place as the principal actors, and you are exposed to seeing costumes intended for major characters, storyboard displays that could provide spoilers for scenes, schedules that map out dates and locations, and even bump into famous actors and directors. It's important to show professionalism here; leave people to get on with their own jobs and don't be seen with your phone out.

Another basic rule to remember for the fittings, is that you need to arrive as a blank canvas, unless told otherwise. Clean hair, minimal or zero makeup, easy to remove clothing, and some of your measurements memorised (shoe size, height, bra size). I once crossed paths with an eager SA who had excitedly turned up to a costume fitting for a new production that was set in the 1500s. Her hair was lovely, but looked like it had been straightened before arriving and was coated in serum. And while the reddish lip stain and dark lined eyes made her look lovely, the makeup definitely wasn't right for the 1500s. Whilst I never got the chance to warn her, I sincerely hope the short-tempered man who did my hair & makeup at the fitting went easy on her when she sat in his chair after I left.

Supplying Own Outfits

There are occasions where the Costume department requires you to bring in selections of your own wardrobe for them to pick from, but usually that's done on the morning of filming. Rarely have I been asked to go see them in advance of the shoot to show my options for them to choose from. When this happens, try to take your own photo so you remember what to bring on the shoot day. Reminders may also be sent beforehand through the agency with a photo or list of what was selected from your options.

Over the years, most artists collate a small wardrobe of things readily available for SA work, and although not necessary, it can sometimes help you book the work. My most-used outfits are the following - **business** (a couple of smart shirts, trousers/skirt, blazer, smart shoes/heels), **wedding guest** suit or dress, and then **basics** such as jeans, jumpers, coats and trainers that are all camera-friendly (no obvious logos, no intricate patterns, a good mixed palette of bold colours and neutral). I never go out and purchase clothes for a specific job, but I look out for things in charity shops, carboot sales, or clothes being given away on Facebook that could expand my wardrobe and become useful later on with the aim of spending as little as possible.

It can be easy to overdo it and bring a suitcase of far too many options in for the team to choose - lots of people do! But I'm slowly learning that it's unnecessary and I now take a couple options only, then let the costume department switch pieces out with their own items, otherwise you'll always be chasing for approval and hardly ever getting it. Every production hates my shirt options anyway, and always gives me one of theirs to wear. So, it's pointless for me to take my whole range of shirts for them to choose from. Instead, I take the plainest one or two just to show willingness, then meekly apologise that I didn't have anything more suitable.

There is also the common phrase you will grow used to hearing: "what you're wearing is fine!". There have been many times I've lugged around a heavy bag of clothing options on public transport and through the streets of London, for it to never even get opened.

8 BEFORE THE SHOOT

For every job you get, there is a whole faff beforehand that everyone goes through, and here is what typically happens before the day of filming:-

1. An availability request will land in your inbox.
2. If selected by production, the agency will message you to say you are booked.
3. Costume fittings are arranged and attended, if required.
4. The agency may contact you again to ask about travel arrangements for the shoot - are you driving or going by public transport?
5. NDA's may be sent for you to sign in advance.

Call details for filming are usually sent the evening before, once the previous shoot day has ended and crew have enough time to sit down and plan out the next day.

There are times where you find yourself put on a pencil instead of being booked. The term "pencil" is increasingly common but is a term that shouldn't really exist. It's when productions want selected SA's to keep the day free in case they are needed, without paying them a retainer fee. This is poor behaviour from AD's or agencies, and we are trying to push against this happening. Myself and other long-term SA's rarely take notice of a pencil. We will say yes to all jobs that come our way until someone actually books us. Then we politely inform the agencies who put us forward for other jobs that we are no longer available, at the earliest opportunity! I was recently on a two-month pencil for a production, which was appalling. Day by day they released me for the following day. By the end of the two months, they had only given me three days of work. You can bet I said yes to other work that cropped up. Pay me a retainer fee if you want me to risk two months of no income.

Waking Up For Work

In my first few years in the industry, I worked a normal day job full time and would fit in a few jobs a year as an extra. What I found most difficult was dealing with the lack of sleep. When my alarm would go off at 4:30am I would shut off the noise and stare at the time on my phone with my eyes still heavy needing sleep. It felt horrifying having to get up, and I used to seriously weigh up whether I should roll over back to sleep and forget about this industry. My stomach would churn at that early hour, and I couldn't think of anything worse than having to get up and drive 90 minutes to spend a chilly day outside in a period costume.

Of course, by now, my alarms have been even earlier – the earliest was 02:30 am. And I wake up quickly and roll straight out to get dressed. I find the excitement of getting to location and having a hot, delicious breakfast a great motivation to get myself ready and in the car. I look forward to each day and can't help but laugh at my younger self for struggling with it so badly. It truly takes some adjusting to.

You should be told in advance whether you need to arrive **camera-ready** for a job which is usually the case on modern day scenes. This could mean hair styled yourself, makeup applied, men clean-shaven, and arriving in one of your costume options. Take that extra amount of preparation time into consideration when you set the alarm. For scenes that are period, you can dress in joggers and arrive with simple clean hair and a washed face ready to be transformed by the Makeup department, although females may be asked to arrive with a light base applied for upper class looks - *light foundation, subtle blush, thin coat of mascara, lip balm*. And actually, men are sometimes given beard instructions like *grow it out or shave it the morning before arriving*. This saves the department time, and they can just top-up the makeup where needed.

Useful Items

Being prepared for filming can make life a lot more comfortable and easier. Particularly in the cold Winter months. The items listed below are things that can help, but it's not necessary to have everything. Just consider the ones you think you'll need the most.

- Water bottle
- Hot drinks flask
- Phone charger
- Portable battery
- Waterproof socks
- Thermal underlayers
- Hand & feet warmers
- Small hot water bottle
- Oversized thick coat
- Suncream, if hot weather
- Book/puzzles/activities (Uno is a hit!)
- Shoe insoles
- Mascara and lip balm, if modern day or upper class
- Travel pillow, if you love a nap

Waterproof socks are a tad pricey, yet so worth it! I had spent many Winters evolving into someone better at dealing with the cold and wet. Every year my stash of warm underlayers grew but I still found some filming days miserable. And it was always when the ground was wet and we're walking through puddles in thin soled, fabric shoes. I began searching Amazon for anything waterproof and was delighted to see that waterproof socks existed. Now I pop them on under my costume socks and can comfortably shoot in all weathers. They're warm too because of the thickness. Remember at the costume fitting to have slightly looser fitting shoes during winter for multiple sock layers.

Many productions give out disposable hand warmers to SA's and crew when the temperatures are low. They will at some point run out, so it's worth keeping a couple packets in your bag in case which easily can be purchased at supermarkets or online or consider buying one of those rechargeable ones to reduce waste.

9 TRAVEL ARRANGEMENTS

Driving really helps and I really wouldn't have half the work I do without it! Saying that, many individuals have managed a good SA life without a car, particularly around cities such as London, Manchester and Liverpool where public transport are reliable throughout the day.

While plenty of crowd bases have been out in rural areas like a muddy farmers field with call times as early as 4am, it's still possible for non-drivers to get some of those jobs. Productions occasionally provide an early coach from Euston station, or minibus shuttles from the closest train station with a slightly later call time.

If you're a driver and have to reach a central location like Holborn in London, it's helpful for drivers to get familiar with cheap or free parking in the outskirts then get a bus or tube to the city location. My favourites are *Morden* or *Wimbledon (for South London)* and *Ealing* or *Park Royal (for West*

London) although it can get busy so best be early. I avoid North and East London personally, because the travel is too far for me. Production may in rare circumstances offer parking in urban areas, but not often because it costs too much to hire spaces for SA cars, Crew cars *and* all the Luton's and vans carrying equipment. Rural locations tend to always have parking provided. It should be mentioned on the booking what assistance there is with shuttles, coaches and parking. Before travelling, check if there are tolls or ULEZ fees to pay. Productions do not reimburse penalty fees.

Long commutes can become problematic when filming days get lengthy, hence why I cap mine at 90 minutes and reject jobs that take longer. We aren't told our hours in advance, but a general rule of thumb is that period dramas could be starting at 5am and finishing 7pm, especially with a large number of crowd. If you live too far away, you may need to consider booking accommodation at your own expense. I've stayed in Airbnb's, Premier Inns, Guest Lodges, with members of my family, and even in my own car plenty of times before. *Word of warning:* lots of confirmed jobs can release you suddenly before the shoot, so it's advisable to hold off booking your accommodation too soon, or at least pay a little more to benefit from the fully refundable option in the event you may need to cancel.

If you get stuck and need to kip in your car overnight, it can be worth talking to security at Crowd base if in a rural area. They're usually happy for people to stay put in the carpark and use the toilet facilities. As long as you aren't building campfires or running around like a maniac in the woods, they don't care.

The journey to where you need to be can be quite tough when it's to a place you've never been before. Particularly when you're being navigated away from motorways into the deep countryside with no sign of life anywhere. Then across the far horizon you'll begin to see a glow of white light coming from the floodlights at unit base. The closer you get to your location, the more bright arrows you'll start seeing with various codes on. Sometimes it will be the initials of the production, other times they will say other things - **LOC** or **SET** to direct people to the place where filming will be. **BASE** is to indicate where the unit base is. **CROWD** directs the crowd to their own area of parking, or to the crowd base. **CARS** directs everyone to parking. It's fairly easy to figure out usually, or there will be strangers lurking in the darkness for you to ask (those strangers are usually Location Marshals or Security personnel).

I made an error one time when two productions were based in the same area as each other. I ended up following the wrong signs and pulled up to a gate where a security guard stood. He asked what I was there for. I said I was a Supporting Artist there for filming, and he let me through. When I parked up in the muddiest field ever with my wheels spinning, I saw in the distance a load of knights on horseback rehearsing a routine with swords. This stopped me in my tracks. I had been hired for a modern-day production playing an armed soldier. After some quick checks on my phone, I realised I was two miles away from where I was supposed to be. I avoided eye contact with the security guard as I departed back out the gate, my car much muddier than when I arrived.

10 A TYPICAL SHOOT DAY

There is a saying that no two days are the same in this industry. It's not *strictly* true, but almost. Some days can feel similar and repetitive, especially when working on a big scene across multiple days or weeks. The more experienced SA's find themselves filming in new places all the time, dressed in different eras, working with fresh faces, and wondering what well-known actors they might see that day, which is why the saying is often said. There can be the excitement of trying to work out what the production actually is, when all we've been given is a codename or abbreviation that provides no answers. It's nice to think ahead to its release and know whether our faces could potentially appear on cinema screens across the country, on streaming platforms with advertisements across social media, or on the television as your family sits with an evening takeaway.

Any form of structure can be beneficial and help us feel somewhat settled into the rhythm of the day. And structure is recognised through repetitively working until you notice a pattern. I am going to try my best to indicate the basic structure of the day so that it hopefully keeps you from feeling overwhelmed on your first job.

This is extremely variable, but I'm giving you the most common structure I've experienced:
6. Arrive at Crowd Base
7. Sign in with the Crowd AD's
8. Get into costume
9. Go through hair & makeup
10. Have breakfast
11. Lineup for checks
12. Continuity photos taken
13. Minibus to location
14. Put personal bags in Crowd Holding
15. Go on set
16. Receive instructions on positions and actions
17. Props are handed out
18. Rehearsal
19. Final Checks
20. Multiple takes and various camera positions
21. Lunch in Crowd Holding (or at Base)
22. Lineup for checks
23. Rehearsal
24. Final Checks
25. Multiple takes and various camera positions
26. 1st AD announces wrap
27. Pick up personal bags from Crowd Holding
28. Minibus back to Crowd Base

29. De-rig costume and hair
30. Sign out with the Crowd AD's

The list may appear daunting to those with little to no experience. It's not necessary to learn it as the AD's will prompt you what to do and when. It can honestly be simplified to *Get Ready - Shoot - Lunch - Shoot - Finish*. This is one of few jobs in the world where you don't have to do much thinking for yourself. The main requirements are to listen and do as you're told (...and don't look into the camera, don't approach the director with a dramatic monologue performance, don't act a diva, and don't livestream around the set like someone got caught doing before). That's literally all.

On set, AD's give **cues** and **actions** to follow, sometimes with a chance for the artist to come up with their own performance that blends in with the scene and doesn't distract from the main focus which is usually action or dialogue centred around main characters. It's all about behaving naturally. If ever in doubt, keep a neutral face, and keep some kind of movement going. There's a good chance you're out of focus. Unless you're the dead body on *Midsomer Murders*, in which case you're going to be fully in focus so you might want to stay still and stop blinking. When I was a kid and spotted the error of a dead body breathing and blinking, I told EVERYONE who would listen.

The number of takes required is a tricky one to estimate. The shot can be complete on its first take, or on the eighteenth take which recently happened! As everyone grumbles and groans back into their first positions to do it all over again, there will be discussions going on among the crew to resolve why they are unable to get the shot they are looking for. Perhaps the director is still trying to squeeze a specific performance out of the actor, maybe there is a problem with cues, the location might be under a flight path with aircraft ruining the sound, someone might have leaned out a nearby window ogling down the lens of the camera, or maybe a mobile phone went off. The thing is, even if they get the shot in the end, they usually have to move the camera into a new position to get more coverage of the same thing. Prepare for a whole day of repetition.

The length of the day can usually be long; however, they can also surprise you and be super short. I did a day as a stand-in on a HBO show and expected it to be a long one. I had barely got through the gate when I was told to drop my bag down and stand in front of the camera. Within an hour, I was finished. Honestly, I had packed my rucksack like I was on a camping trip with spare socks, a phone charger, and a waterproof jacket in case it rained during the twelve hours I had expected to be there. They only needed me to test some lighting and a couple of camera moves, and I was still paid for the whole day. Result. Then there's the 45 minutes I had on set in the hospital bed that I mentioned earlier. Easy.

Making Friends

If you ever get a job on a production, be sure to chat to other SA's if you get the chance. It's the most fascinating thing. On surface level, a crowd of extras can appear mundane with the only evidence of life being sparked by the appearance of food and snacks. If you look below the surface, you'll discover that most of these people have the most fascinating lives. Not just the stories they can tell you of the productions they've worked on, but some of them have really interesting day jobs. Many times, I've wandered past them silently on camera giving a polite nod or engaging in mimed conversation, only to discover later on between setups that they are a retired police officer, a tech company owner, a military reserve, or a government worker. Maybe you'll meet a person who bizarrely knows some of your family members – that's happened too! I've also been introduced to many creative individuals who turned out to be experienced singers, comedians, musicians, photographers, painters, independent filmmakers, authors and more!

People love to help each other out with advice and tips. I saw a professional masseuse giving an elderly woman an upper back massage to help relieve a problem she was having, and he had no expectation of anything in return. I had an accountant talk to me in great detail about tax and the things I can claim back as expenses which I never realised. Another time, I befriended a girl, and it turned out she was the daughter of the 1st AD. She introduced me to him, and he remembered my name for the rest of the day and gave me a doughnut out of the snack box which was meant for crew only. To be fair a lot of the AD team are brilliant with remembering names of SA's. It never fails to amaze me how they do that, and it is a skill I definitely lack.

Bottom Of The Hierarchy

With the number of crowd the AD's have to deal with, it comes as no surprise that we get herded around and spoken to like we're at school. It's a management system that is at times annoying for us, but usually effective. However, SA's can also come across moments where, despite your professionalism and doing things correctly, you will find yourself at the receiving end of an unhappy AD. I was once sitting in the makeup chair when the phone rang in my pocket displaying a phone number I didn't recognise. On answering, a panicked voice asked where I was. Now this could have been anyone, but I could sense this was to do with the filming and was either an agent or AD. "I'm at my filming job," I responded vaguely, unsure of how much detail they were expecting from me. The other person was confused. "Get here as quick as you can, please!" I turn to look over at the sign-in desk to see a woman on the phone. "I'm in the makeup chair," waving wildly so she could see. "You didn't sign in." Even as she said that a look of recognition crossed her face. Probably remembering how just thirty minutes ago I had gone up to her on arrival and given my name. "Remember to sign in each morning," and she hung up. She was still blaming me even though we both knew it was her own mistake. I let it slide knowing she would forget all about me and stressfully be trying to figure out who she had accidentally signed in that was now a no-show. People actually do that, you know. They just don't show up. Likely because they rolled back over in bed to sleep.

Another time I messaged an AD warning him I might be ten minutes late. We also spoke briefly on the phone before my calltime as he asked for an update. It turns out I was only four minutes late. But when I got there, he was fuming. "I've already complained to the agency." This annoyed me but I wasn't going to retaliate because he'd send me home and I was due to be earning a good amount of money for this nightshoot. "Okay," I responded calmly, which I think infuriated him even more. The next evening the agency phoned saying that I had turned up late and not informed the AD. I explained that he had been aware beforehand, and that I was only minutes late for reasons beyond my control. They didn't care. My name was probably highlighted as *one to watch out for, they cause trouble.* Sigh. I've seen too many people retaliate which escalates it out to something much worse. They might find themselves kicked off the production or even the agency books for something that probably wasn't their fault to begin with.

I'm not passing this on to scare you! 97% of the time things go smoothly, and everyone's in a good mood with intentions of keeping the vibes up across the whole day. As long as you can look past the demands that make you feel like a child... *Line up. Hands out your pockets. Spit that gum out, Victorian peasants didn't have gum. Put your phone away in your bag. Stop talking. Ask before disappearing to the toilet...* Yes, boss!

11 INTERACTIONS WITH CREW

There are a huge number of crew roles on set, and I still don't know what all of them do. But these are the ones that SA's commonly interact with, and I've also mentioned when you might come across them:

Crowd AD's - These guys are typically the first point of contact for SA's on arrival to a job, aside from Security or Location Marshals who will be sorting the parking. Crowd AD's get us through the works at base, ensure we're fed + watered, and escort us to set.

3rd AD's - When we are on the set, the 3rd AD's take charge of us, informing us of the backstory of the scene and what our expected reactions should be. They will provide us with directions and actions and make the important selections such as who gets featured if this wasn't decided in advance. Crowd AD's and Runners may also be around to help them.

1st AD - The smooth running of the set will be down to the 1st AD who is responsible for keeping everything to schedule and making sure everything is done safely. They will be the voice on set you'll hear a lot with main cues such as *turnover/roll camera* for the crew, followed shortly after with *background action* for the extras… and *action*. The 1st AD talks broadly to the SA's a lot to keep momentum and energy up and pass along notes from either the Director about performance or from the Script Supervisor about continuity - alternatively they may have the 3rd AD pass along those notes directly to the relevant people.

Director - This is a rare interaction as the Director is usually focused on the main cast, leaving direction of the SA's in the trusted hands of the AD team. However, sometimes the Director may weigh in with suggestions and direction to individual SA's or groups.

Props - Objects for SA's to handle such as cameras, bags, baskets, newspapers, coins, tickets etc are handed out by the Props department. They may take photographs of the SA holding the item for continuity and so that it can be tracked down quickly if it goes missing and ends up away from the set by accident.

Armourer - For artists who are handling weapons such as guns and swords, you will be under supervision and guidance from an Armourer who is in charge of the weapon. Safety is a huge priority for them, and they won't tolerate any messing around. Sometimes you will go through a training session with them before filming to ensure you handle the weapon correctly.

Makeup - you will see the Makeup department often, including at your fittings, while you're getting ready for the shoot, in lineups, and on set. They will take continuity photos of you almost daily. Makeup artists are usually up for a good chat when you're in the chair and I've found them to be a friendly bunch.

Costume - You will also be seeing the Costume department often at your fittings, while you're getting ready for the shoot, in lineups, and on set. They also like to take continuity photos daily. Make sure you have your costume number ready! If it's the first day and you don't know it, they'll tell you and expect you to remember it for next time.

Caterers - You'll get to eat the *hopefully* delicious food made by the team of caterers. They may have the food prepackaged, or they may serve up by request. Puddings are usually fantastic and offer generous servings. Order quickly though. They won't stand for hesitation when there's hundreds of other people behind you in the queue. It may please you to know that the next chapter is dedicated solely to food, simply because it's what I look forward to most in the day!

12 MEALTIMES

Most jobs where filming is taking place will feed us. Costume fittings and BBC jobs (like *Eastenders* and *Casualty*) typically won't. I've also experienced some filming days where I've been asked to bring in my own lunch which they paid me extra for as compensation. This has only been on very small shoots where there weren't enough cast & crew numbers to make it worth hiring an entire catering team.

For bigger productions, it's almost a guarantee we'll be fed, but I like to read every sentence of the confirmation email from the agency just in case they mention that the calltime is after breakfast or there's no meals provided. One of my biggest filming fears is that my stomach will rumble during a take with hundreds of people in the room. That happened to me on a student film once. My other fear is that I accidentally make a take unusable by perhaps falling over or dropping something loudly. This, too, happened when I played a restaurant waiter for a TV show, and I dropped a load of cutlery during an intense conversation between the main cast. I was removed from my spot after that and have never said yes to the role of a waiter since.

Back to topic. Let's start with breakfast. What a feast. Sometimes the catering team doesn't even put a menu board out, because if you want something, they most likely have it.

After nine years of opting for the trusty full English breakfast, I got fed up and started glancing curiously as to what others were eating. Some had porridge with berries. Others were eating toast. Healthier individuals would eat through a medley of fruits. I noticed some of the makeup girls would ask for avocado on toast. I would recoil inside wondering why they would choose something so weird when hash browns were an option. I'd never actually tried avocado at that point and thought it looked rank. I got to a point where I started experimenting with orders. I tried the porridge. It was surprisingly very good and kept me going right up until lunchtime.

But my best breakfast was on a day where I thought I was going to miss this mealtime altogether. I was working a job where I was being held in the costume department for a long time while they faffed over minor details. The catering team was due to stop serving at any moment. When the AD came in, I told her slightly panicked that I hadn't eaten yet. She kindly reassured me that I won't die of starvation on her watch, and she set off to go grab me something to eat. Minutes later I was released by the costume team, and the AD came and handed me a container. I quickly sat on the dining bus to eat, already aware that we were heading to set any moment. The food in that container was incredible! A soft bagel filled with chilli avocado and poached egg. Definitely not something I would have considered ordering for myself, but it was delicious.

On my next job I hesitantly approached the catering truck at breakfast wondering if I could recreate the order, or whether they would tell me to get lost and choose something normal. *Do you have bagels?* To my surprise they nodded. *Is it possible to have that with avocado, poached egg and a hash brown please?* Within seconds I had the perfect bagel handed to me. That has become my new favourite breakfast until I grow bored of that one too. I'll admit that because of the 14-hour days we were working on this production, I followed it up with a bowl of porridge, another hash brown, and a yoghurt. My next breakfast-goal is to learn quantity-control.

I actually almost forgot to mention what a terrible breakfast can look like. Sometimes, when there isn't time to line all the SA's up at the catering truck, an apologetic crew member will arrive at crowd base armed with large black boxes. They will enter to a muttering of moans from the experienced extras who know what this means. Inside are small foil packages containing dry baps with either sausage, bacon, or veggie sausages. They're usually cold by the time they reach us and are difficult to eat without having a sauce of some kind in it. Anyway, that's it for breakfast. I didn't think I would have this much to write about, but it's one of the highlights of the day for me.

Lunchtime stresses me out. You don't know what will be on offer unless a kind crew member reads the list to you, and the queue moves very slowly. If there's a menu out on display, you'll typically see a meat option (like spaghetti bolognaise, lasagne, various cuts of meat), a fish option, and a veggie option. The industry has also improved in that you won't be shunned for having other dietary requirements. They can usually accommodate vegan or gluten-free requests and other types too, although this may need mentioning to an AD at the start of the day. After being handed your main meal in a container, you'll likely have a whole assortment of sides to serve up for yourself – leafy salads, coleslaw, breads, and cheese boards. If you want to skip this, you can beeline straight towards pudding. There are multiple options available here too, usually about three to choose from. The ones I see most often are sponge cakes, brownies, and cheesecakes. The amount of time available to eat the food is a tricky one. On a **Standard Day**, you are given an hour to eat your meal. If that hour is interrupted to return to work, then the production has to pay you a meal penalty. If the day is a **Continuous Day**, you might only eat a mouthful before being rushed back. It once took me three hours to finish my lunch because I kept getting called back to set.

Now onto the mid-afternoon snacks. There's usually an assortment of sandwiches for us to choose from about mid-afternoon or close to wrap time. I look for Egg Mayo usually. If we're lucky, there will be boxes of crisps and even chocolate bars and fruit available for us to choose from. People laugh at how SA's swarm round the food like starved animals, but if you aren't quick, you'll lose out to the greedy people who grab multiple crisps and chocolate bars to stash into their bag. I'm not kidding. I despise the people who do this. They can be joyfully chatting to you one minute, then fighting to grab as many snacks as possible the next. It's embarrassing to watch, and I feel sorry for the runner who is quickly trying to escape the oncoming herd.

13 KEEPING TRACK OF JOBS

It can be hard for individuals to keep track of days they've worked or got coming up! There may be circumstances where the production requires you for further filming dates, so you may get requests to come back again! On one job, I was initially booked to work three days; they kept asking me back, and by the time the production had ended, I had clocked up twenty-five days. These extra days can be a bit of a muddle when they're spread out with various other bits of work in between. But it's better than having the reverse happen - a block booking which slowly depletes into just a handful of days worked.

A notebook or spreadsheet is a handy way to track jobs, earnings and payments. Everyone seems to have different preferences and variations with their own headings and content. While some prefer to handwrite their jobs down in diary form, I prefer a **Google Sheets** document which can be used on mobile as well as desktop. I'm unable to print a screenshot of my table due to the information being enough to break NDA, but I will list the column titles and example content for what I'd put in them (this is a fictional production I made up in a fictional location to use as an example):

Date: 04/01/2024
Agency: Casting Collective
Production: Summer Harvest, Film
Role: Farmer
Call: 05:30
Wrap: 18:45
Location: Blue Farm, Surrey
Gross: £275.15
Net: £226.99

This is essentially the kind of key information you want to note down.

My real spreadsheet is colourful with the date column changing to a new colour every time we go into a new tax year. And I've included further columns to track deductions, production company names, and additional expenses that may crop up. I also added check boxes, so I can tick it off when I receive payments into my bank account, allowing me to see at a glance which productions I need to chase up with the agency. And, on Google Sheets I discovered that I could add a note which becomes visible when you hover over a cell, so I added a note to the *Gross* cells which shows a breakdown of the payment (day rate, holiday, overtime, travel, supplementary payments etc).

At one point I started a spreadsheet to track availability requests, pencils and bookings but this proved too time-consuming, and I gave up after a month. Now I just pop them into my phone calendar, then delete them if I get released. My phone is full of abbreviations that would only make sense to myself and other SA's. No use typing out *Casting Collective* over and over when I can shorten it to *CC*. Many of the common abbreviations are listed toward the end of this document so you don't feel like you're out of the loop.

14 FINANCES

Apologies in advance for all the random numbers I throw at you in this section… It can be a lot to take in, but hopefully I've simplified my explanations enough to help!

Depending on the agency, you should get the breakdown of everything you earned for the filming day within hours or days working, including an opportunity to query if the earnings don't look correct. The agency then invoices the production on your behalf to receive the payment. The agency will keep their deductions (commission plus VAT), then transfer the rest into your bank account. On average it takes 6-8 weeks to receive payment after the filming day, but there are instances where wait times are much shorter or much longer. Artists tend to start chasing up with the agency after eight weeks have lapsed if no updates have been sent out.

The amount earned for each day depends on the rate the production follows. Typically, a production is on **FAA** or **Equity/PACT** rates with the former reaching higher figures. There are also differing rates for **BBC** and **ITV** just to make matters even more confusing, not to mention the pay difference between commercials, music videos and photographic jobs. The next two calculations will show you how payments are decided on for feature films and television, then I will provide some links to help inform you of exact figures.

A standard day without supplementary payments will look like this calculation:

DAY RATE + HOLIDAY PAY + TRAVEL = GROSS AMOUNT

And what goes into your bank account will look like this calculation:

GROSS AMOUNT - DEDUCTIONS = NET AMOUNT

The exact up-to-date figures can be found on the *BECTU* website found on any search engine or by using this web address:
https://bectu.org.uk/get-involved-in-the-union/ratecards/
- then scrolling down to the section labelled *FAA Background Artistes* where a downloadable rate card is available. You will be able to see all the supplementary

payments that can top up earnings to an attractive lump sum, including overtime, meal penalties, early morning travel, use of skills etc. The best day for me was one that included the supplements for **overtime + early call + turnaround + stand-in + late lunch** which more than tripled a standard day amount.

Casting Collective also has a great page on their website with all the current rates and information in an easy format right here:
https://www.castingcollective.co.uk/production/pay-rates - You can find additional information about projects that don't fall under FAA rates and see how different job types compare.

There is also a handy little website designed by a current SA called <u>casting.me</u> (just type that into the URL bar), and there you can input information from your day such as calltime, wrap time, travel etc and it will tell you the amount you should be receiving for the day. I don't know if that site has been updated to the 2024 rates yet.

My highest gross amount for one day of filming has been £384.63 on a period production and my lowest has been £81.09 on a TV show where we were only required for a half day. This is before deductions. For costume fittings, I tend to get upwards of £72.89 as they are known as a shift call *(up to four hours)*. Covid tests used to have similar payments to Costume Fittings, but thankfully the requirements for these tests are no longer the norm in the industry. It used to be frustrating blocking out multiple days in the week from potential jobs to have numerous Covid tests before every fitting and filming date with only half a day's pay. I'm in a better financial position now that those are gone.

Here is an **example breakdown** of a day's pay for working on a feature film located in Central London on the FAA 2024 rates:

BASIC DAY RATE	£105.09
HOLIDAY	£11.31
TRAVEL - CATEGORY A	£14.69
OVERTIME	£54.65
LATE LUNCH	£21.86
TOTAL	**£207.60**

Travel payments are determined by the location you have to get to. Central London locations get the lowest travel payments (Category A), even if you are travelling all the way from Gloucestershire to be there. Areas further out can attract higher travel payments. All of this should be explained easier in the links provided above. Please note, I'm unsure how it works up North as I've only ever worked down South.

If you're still wondering what *Late Lunch* is, that is a meal penalty given to you if it has been more than six hours since your calltime and you still haven't broken for lunch. I have received this payment quite a few times, especially when calltimes have been early.

Tax and National Insurance

Individuals should conduct their own thorough research and consider professional advice in case of errors in this section. I'm not a financial advisor.

There are two types of employment discussed here.

A. **PAYE** where you receive payslips from an *employer* or any *companies you freelance for* with tax, national insurance, student loans deducted.

B. **Self-Employed** where *you* inform HMRC of your earnings and expenses through a self-assessment on their Government Gateway portal.

Being a supporting artist, you must register as self-employed with HMRC if you start earning more than £1,000 per year, and declare your earnings annually through self-assessment, even if you made a loss. This is to avoid fines and possible legal action. There are thresholds where you will start to owe **Tax**. This used to include National Insurance, but I believe the requirement to pay National Insurance has recently been removed for people who run their own business. The amount of tax you owe will be calculated for you, with a deadline to pay it. You can choose to pay National Insurance voluntarily at that stage; you need 35 years of qualifying payments to receive the full state pension at retirement age. **Tip: set aside a portion of your earnings into an easy access savings account to ensure you can make end-of-year payments!**

If, like me, you are in both of the above types of employment *(PAYE and Self-Employed)*, it's good to know that PAYE employment will automatically have the figures added to your government gateway and you do not need to do anything other than add your self-employed work and make the necessary payments. Many people use accountancy services as they are able to help with putting in expenses, but it can be done without one as long as you have researched enough to understand what you're doing, and keep good records stored in case of an investigation against you.

GOVERNMENT GATEWAY SETUP:
https://www.access.service.gov.uk/login/signin/creds?ao
c=N

HOW TO FILL OUT SELF-ASSESSMENT:
https://www.moneyhelper.org.uk/en/work/self-
employment/how-to-fill-in-a-self-assessment-tax-return

Expenses

Make sure to carefully document every income and expense with evidence in the form of receipts, chits, remittances etc.

This is a general idea of expenses you can claim on your tax return:

- Uniforms and clothes that can't be used for everyday wear
- Parking, tolls, ULEZ, mileage
- Union fees
- DBS Certificate costs
- Portion of phone & internet costs
- Equipment used for self-tapes
- Accommodation

Again, it's a good idea to research and get professional advice. There may be many more to add to this list that I'm not aware of or have forgotten to include.

15 SECRECY ON HIGH-PROFILE JOBS

It is normal to have no idea what project you are booked for. Productions regularly use code names to maintain secrecy about storylines, characters, casting decisions and to retain audience anticipation and allow the project to be marketed in a strategic way for best financial results. It can also avoid unwanted attention from paparazzi, fans and people living near filming locations. It is sometimes completely possible to find out what the real project is through an internet search or on social media pages for cast, crew & SA's. And you can bet that fans and the Media will find things out anyway.

I once found an image of myself in a local newspaper standing next to other SA's when I worked on an old episode of Doctor Who at a time where people were excited about a new actor filling the shoes of the title role. We were filming in some dense woodland with fencing around the area and had our phones taken away from us to avoid leaks, but some paparazzi had found a gap to shoot through using long lenses. It baffled me how they had found our location or why they were so interested.

Whilst it can be common for people within the industry to whisper filming secrets amongst each other, it is poor practice to share this information to 'outsiders' and is a clause that you'll usually find included in the Non-Disclosure Agreements you'll be signing. When crew members and SA's are approached on location by members of the public and asked about the filming, the default response should be along the lines of *"I'm sorry, I can't say"* to avoid breaking the terms of the NDA. If you feel uncomfortable, anxious or unsure, you can direct them to ask security who will be dotted around the perimeter in uniform or hi-vis jackets.

So, while I can't expose the code names for anything I've personally worked on (due to signing NDA's and because future seasons sometimes re-use the same codename), I can share the more famous one's from older productions that can be found through an easy Google search:

- *Planet Ice = Titanic*
- *Artemis = The Hunger Games*
- *Group Hug = Avengers*
- *Wham! = Deadpool*
- *Prime Directive = Transformers*
- *Incident on 57th Street = Harry Potter & the Chamber of Secrets*
- *Fiona's Letter = Interstellar*

- *Rory's First Kiss = The Dark Knight*
- *Oliver's Arrow = Inception*
- *Blue Harvest = Star Wars: Return of the Jedi*
- *Paradox = Back to the Future Part II*

Sometimes codenames have relevance to the production and other times they can be completely random and fun which works to avoid attention for something that is being made by a famous director or about a sensitive topic. For example, James Cameron wanted to keep the project of Titanic under wraps, but with lots of their filming activity happening around Nova Scotia it made sense to create a fictional project called *Planet Ice* to throw people off the scent that a film was in the works about the ship, Titanic.

When you come to do filming on high-profile productions, you'll find that you may be required to hand your phone over to a member of security so it can get locked away. This feels like a lack of trust, but there have been some SA's in the past who have published images before official announcements have been made about the production, and there was a rumoured incident where someone live streamed a tour around the Eastenders set whilst the crew were setting up for an episode.

16 RESILIENCE

The industry can be a volatile one. It came to a halt during the height of the Covid-19 pandemic, and many were surprised when the film and television industry went on lockdown. A lot of people at the time were self-employed or freelance. There were financial schemes available, but I couldn't wrap my head around how they survived. Apparently, this was a time when a lot of people took the opportunity to retire early from the industry. Things moving forward were very uncertain, so it made sense for some to jump ship. I found myself waiting for emails from agencies, or crew posts on Facebook with information on when things would start filming again. And it did eventually. But I had no idea that my Netflix job on Saturday 22nd February 2020 would be the last time I stepped onto a professional set for 15 months. Cue a new era for me working in retail and hospitality!

My first professional film and television job back after the covid pandemic was for a BBC series in May 2021. It was insanely nerve-wracking for me as the filming day approached. Up until this job, I had never taken a Covid Test, never been around large groups of people since the virus began, didn't know what to expect, and had lost some of the confidence I used to have as a Supporting Artist. The production was incredibly strict and had procedures for us to follow - get tested before filming, isolate until day of filming, wear a mask at all times except when cameras are rolling, avoid facing in the direction of cast members to minimise their risk of potential exposure, keep a minimum of two metres distance from everyone, and sanitise yourself and anything you touch. If a single case of the virus was found among the cast & crew, the production would immediately shut down. That's why a video surfaced of Tom Cruise losing his temper at crew on his Mission Impossible franchise. Back then, breaking Covid-19 protocols had serious and costly consequences for productions and individuals. It was a crazy time!

The industry was again affected in the Summer of 2023 when two American unions, the Writers Guild of America and SAG-AFTRA, went on strike. This had quite an impact on the UK where many American productions shoot. Feature films and shows stopped production, putting crew members, actors, background actors, caterers etc in limbo with little work available. The reasons for the strikes were wholly necessary, and despite being in a difficult situation dealing with a sudden drop in work, myself and others completely agreed with the reasons behind the strikes, particularly as the results of a strong negotiation will benefit us as well and the future of SA's.

Throughout times where the industry broke down, many individuals as mentioned retired early, changed careers, took up temporary work in "normal" jobs or started their own businesses. Being able to financially support yourself in this delicate line of work is incredibly important. It might be the case that you go a full year without any extra work. Personally, I had to consider a part time weekend job in retail to help with my bills and rent as the strikes happened. I also currently write in my spare time with the hope that it will provide some residual income. You'll meet people who have additional jobs in events, teaching, call centres, their own business, or are currently studying. It's interesting hearing others' stories.

If I can work a minimum of 10 days a month, then I've earned everything I need for the month to cover basic living expenses. Any extra earnings go into an easy access savings account to cover the shortfall on months where I haven't earned enough and will be available for me when I need to make annual payments for things like taxes, national insurance, car insurance, MOT's, servicing and anything else. Personal money management is a seriously under-taught area, but I'm happy to see it creeping into school curriculums nowadays. I'm grateful I had the common sense to teach myself in my twenties and learn everything I could about finances.

A forgotten area that doesn't get enough discussion, is pension contributions. Making an effort to contribute something into a pension pot would be wise and has become a focus of mine this year. I've neglected this in the past, but recently started making small monthly contributions to increase my pot ready for retirement. It's not a lot as I am a low earner, but starting early and being consistent helps, so I'm trying to take this more seriously.

Another area of resilience is mental health. The long days and last-minute cancellations can really take a toll on top of other stresses in life. It can feel personal, and many individuals have shown offence by the constant rejection, even venting blame towards agencies. Those with pre-existing mental health conditions may find themselves facing triggers, or they may experience the opposite and find this work the escapism from real life they need - that's how it is for me anyway! But I have found myself turning down social events and family get-togethers because I want to keep the day free for potential filming due to being anxious and stressed about money. And despite working on set with hundreds of others around you, it can sometimes be a lonely lifestyle to keep up. The topic of mental health is quite a strong one in the film & tv industry with more acknowledgement towards it in recent times and resources available. Check with your union and don't forget to look into various forms of help through the government, local councils and charities if you think you need support

17 TRADE UNION

Supporting Artists in the UK have two unions available to them. The first one is the **FAA branch of BECTU** dedicated to SA's in London and surrounding counties. It costs £5 per month using the discount code - ***PBFABRAP***. The other is **Equity,** which is typically for Actors, Dancers, and any SA's outside the London catchment. Some people like to sign up with both, but others prefer to use the one whose rates they are normally paid. *Agencies should be informing artists whether the offered work is on FAA or Equity rates, or other rates such as BBC/ITV.*

The unions can provide legal assistance relating to issues that the agency has been unable to resolve and can have great influence over productions, which is why agencies recommend that individuals sign up. It's not compulsory to become a union member, but it might just save you in the future. They also have great schemes available with discounts in travel, beauty, technology, insurance etc. The benefits of being part of the union can save you far more than the monthly cost, making it good financial sense to join. And it's those guys who fight for pay increases and better working conditions. The more people sign up, the stronger our standing will be. We are integral to the shoot, but we are also easy to replace, so it's good to have an organisation fighting in our corner.

How To Join BECTU

This step-by-step guidance will assist you in joining the FAA branch of BECTU:-

https://bectu.org.uk/join/

1. Fill your personal details out on the first page.
2. Are you currently freelance? Click **"Yes"**
3. Job Title: type **"Supporting Artist"**
4. Sector: type **"FABR"**
5. Input additional personal information
6. Promotional Code: type **"PBFABRAP"**
7. Check the box saying Direct Debit - £10.00 (when you click to the next page then return to previous page, this will have been lowered to **£5.00 monthly**)
8. Input bank details to set up your monthly direct debit
9. Success! You will receive a confirmation email, then a welcome pack in the post.

You will now have an account set up to log into and be given a BECTU number which identifies you to them. So, if you have any problems with a job that can't be resolved through the agency, you can now contact BECTU with that number for advice.

How To Join Equity

You first need to meet eligibility requirements to join this union. Individuals need to have earned £500 from the industry with acceptable evidence (for Supporting Artists I believe your chits or remittances are enough along with the dates worked).

This is the link to get further information and to join:

https://www.equity.org.uk/join-us

Equity is simpler to sign up with and doesn't require any special promo codes. The cost of subscription is based on how much you earn per year. The fee will be upped to **£168 per year** from 1st February 2024 if earnings are under £40k.

If you believe that union membership isn't for you and you'd rather save your money, I'd recommend at least having discussions with other members next time you're on-set to consider all facts and make the best decision for yourself.

18 TRANSITIONING TO CAST OR CREW

Some people use SA work as a gateway to learn about the Film & TV industry or specific departments before settling into careers as a Crew member or Actor. It can certainly give you an advantage to understand the roles on-set, the typical workday, and get used to sets, equipment, even radio etiquette if you've been a stand-in.

Your on-set experience may offer a helping hand when competing against other entry-level people who have perhaps paid to attend courses that teach what SA's gain for free. When applying for jobs as a Runner or Location Marshal, you can highlight transferable skills and experience which could make you more desirable than someone who's graduated university and never been in a studio, on location, or navigated Crowd bases and Unit bases before.

Transitioning to becoming an actor is rarer and is yet one of the more desired paths. Talking to other artists, you'll discover that many of them went to drama school or regularly attend acting classes. While it's true that many famous people such as Brad Pitt were once extras, they also studied for their craft, had contacts in the industry, or got lucky during a time when the industry wasn't so easily accessible. Nowadays, Universities and Drama Schools churn out acting students by the thousands each year, all chasing the same line of work. Many of them are inexperienced in real set-life. We, at least, have that sort of experience. Not to say that it's impossible to go into professional acting, but there are a lot of people with the same dream. If you think you can achieve it, then give it a go and good luck, but stay humble!

19 RESOURCES

Some of these resources may be helpful to those considering a life as an SA and can offer places for advice and guidance from those with experience.

Social Media

- **Heavy Pencil**, *Facebook* - a community of SA's who share advice, conversations, and vent frustrations
- **Crew Rooms**, *Facebook* - for finding short term accommodation
- **SA Digs UK**, *Facebook* - a new group recently set up for further short-term accommodation
- **TV & Film Extra Group**, *Facebook* - community group
- **Wales & West SAs**, *Facebook* - community group
- **London Actors, Stunts, Spacts & Supporting Artist**, *Facebook*

- **Casting Collective Supporting Artiste Group,** *Facebook*
- **Piece of Cake Casting SA Group,** *Facebook*
- **The Hall of Shame - Rogue Casting Agencies,** *Facebook*
- **Movie Set Memes,** *Facebook* - for light-hearted film set banter
- **SA Carpool,** *WhatsApp* - for sharing rides, having a chit chat, getting advice
- **recycledmoviecostumes,** *Instagram* - if you are interested in seeing how costumes are recycled between productions

There may be many more I don't know about. These ones were discovered through general searches and through word-of-mouth while working on jobs.

SA's also tend to set up WhatsApp chats for particular productions if they are part of the core-SA team and work many days alongside each other. It can be a place to catch-up, discuss concerns, share car rides, or even to arrange a reunion to see the finished film in the cinema. These groups aren't affiliated with the production itself.

Other Handy Resources

- **What3Words:** https://what3words.com/ - Available on desktop and as an app. Great for navigating to the precise location you need to be at. More and more productions nowadays are using what3words so it's good to have it downloaded on a smartphone ready.

- **TV Watercooler:** https://tvwatercooler.org/ - A list of rogue productions, companies, and individuals to avoid working with. It will detail the concerns about them. This may be useful to those who are looking for opportunities on low-budget or independent projects.

- **The Film & Television Charity:** https://filmtvcharity.org.uk/ - I believe this charity is mostly for crew, but a handy resource if you find yourself crossing over to that side of the camera.

- **Shout (resource for Mental Health):** https://giveusashout.org/ - A free 24/7 service that can provide mental health support for those suffering distress. The service is provided over text to anyone resident in the UK.

- **Citizens Advice:** https://www.citizensadvice.org.uk/ - A handy service that can provide resources and support on a range of topics from housing, work, debt, health, and benefits plus more.

20 FAQ's

Will I meet famous people? Sometimes, yes! I've met many famous actors & directors over the years with some of them making polite conversations with myself and other SA's. The unspoken rule is to not talk to them unless they speak to you first.

Is the money good? You can earn more in a day than you would in a normal minimum wage job. And with specialist skills and upgrades for being featured, doubling and standing-in, you can be on hundreds per day. However, the consistency of work is tricky.

Can I make a living from this? It's rare to find anyone who relies solely on the income from this work. Most people supplement this with shift work, part time jobs, pension income, or studying. It's not a stable source of money as the frequency of work can be low.

How can I make the most money? As well as capitalising on learning new skills, consider making yourself desirable for period dramas where the long hours of getting ready can mean lots of overtime pay.

Is the job difficult? The hardest part is getting yourself there! The job itself should be easy enough if you listen well and can follow instructions.

Are SA's classed as self-employed? Yes - we are responsible for our own tax and national insurance.

Can I turn work down? When you get availability requests, it is absolutely fine to say no to them. Agencies understand that we all have lives outside the industry or are working with other agencies on different projects. There is no need to provide an explanation.

What if I said yes to work, but now I'm unavailable? If you really cannot do a pencilled or booked date, a polite explanation and apology to the agency will be the best course of action. Try not to let this become a common occurrence. If you were already booked and fitted for a job which you then cancelled, the agency may remove you from their books, or operate a three-strikes policy where you get two chances before being removed.

What if multiple jobs have booked me on the same day? The rule of thumb is to be loyal to the job that booked you first. Informing agencies that you are no longer available should be done as soon as possible to avoid double-booking. If this has already happened, the only thing you can do is to apologise to the agency who was second in line and try not to let that happen again. A double-booked scenario requires immediate action so that the second agency can find a replacement for you in time.

Do I need acting experience? No, anyone can do this. As long as you can behave naturally without drawing attention to yourself, you'll be okay.

Can I use professional headshots? You can use them in your main photos if you have them. But don't use them in the *selfie upload* section as these require natural photos in natural lighting and need updating regularly.

Does Covid still play a big role? There are still Covid departments on a few productions, but for the most part, the tests and masks are long gone.

What if I become unwell on set? Inform an AD. There will be a medic available to assist. As well as a hefty first aid kit, they also tend to carry painkillers, sanitary towels and sunscreen. Health & safety is a huge priority in the film and television industry. Nobody will be mad at you for becoming unwell.

Will I be credited at the end? Usually not, unless you were important to the story.

Do SA's get invited to film premieres or wrap parties? The number of individuals involved in creating a film is colossal. From development and pre-production, all the way to post-production, distribution and marketing. Many people, including SA's, realistically won't receive an invite. I have received a wrap party invite only one time! That was for a small independent film that was being submitted to film festivals. I only worked on it for one day as background, so it came as a surprise, and I didn't attend.

21 COMMON TERMINOLOGY

10-1 Pronounced "ten one". The code means toilet break.

AGENCY Agencies are the middleman who supply productions with extras.

ANTAGONIST The enemy or villain of the story.

BACKGROUND ACTION The cue for SA's to begin their action prior to main 'action' being called.

BACK-TO-ONES Resetting actors, SA's, camera & lighting positions back to their first positions.

BALLS & CHARTS Recording of sources of light ready for post-production visual effects.

BLOCKING Deciding where actors and SA's will be positioned and the path they will travel.

BLUE/GREEN SCREEN Used as a backdrop to film action which is later composited over a different background.

BOLLYWOOD The Indian filmmaking industry.

BOOM Long pole holding a microphone to pick up dialogue and other audio.

BROKEN LUNCH When lunch has not been provided within the FAA's recommended timeframe.

BUYOUT A lump sum amount of money instead of regular repeat fees.

CALL DETAILS Expected arrival time, address, emergency contacts, and other important information.

CALLSHEET/SIDES A condensed document containing the schedule, contact info, script etc.

CHIT Paperwork provided at the end of the day/after the shoot.

CLAPPERBOARD/SLATE A black & white board 'clapped' in front of the camera displaying information useful for editors.

CRAFT A supply of drinks and snacks to order. Usually reserved only for cast & crew.

COMMISSION A deduction which pays the agency for finding work on your behalf.

COMPOSITING A post-production process where filmed elements are layered over each other.

CONTINUITY Maintaining seamless consistency between different shots, so the final edit works well.

CONTINUOUS DAY A seven-hour day before overtime starts, without a dedicated hour for lunch.

CRANE Usually refers to an extendable arm 'driven' into position holding a camera.

CROWD BASE Usually a large marquee where SA's get ready in costume & makeup.

DBS CERTIFICATE An official record of a person's criminal convictions.

DE-RIG Removing and returning costumes and hair pieces at the end of the day.

DINING BUS Literally a stationary bus to eat on and can double as a holding area.

DOUBLE A person substituting in place of an actor for a shot.

END BOARD Using the clapperboard at the end of the take before cutting the camera, instead of at the start.

EXPOSITION A wide shot to set the scene and let audiences see the surroundings.

FEATURED Being distinctive on screen and helping the story.

FINAL CHECKS When Makeup and Costume have one last opportunity for adjustments before the camera starts recording.

GROSS AMOUNT Total sum of earnings before any deductions are made.

HOLDING An area near to set for SA's to rest when not required.

HONEYWAGON Portable toilets.

LAVALIER/TIE MIC Small microphone attached to a performer powered by a hidden battery pack.

LINEUP A line of SA's who get checked by Makeup and Costume before travelling to holding/set/location.

LOCATION Where filming activity takes place.

LOCATION MARSHAL Assisting around locations and managing members of the public.

MANITOU Tall lights that are 'driven' into position and extended to desired height.

MIMING Faking the conversation or action.

NET AMOUNT A final amount of money after deductions which is paid to the worker.

NIGHTSHOOT When filming is shifted so that hours are overnight instead of during the day.

NON-PERFORMANCE A broad term covering costume fittings or rehearsals.

POP/WE GOT POP A platform which rebranded to become Entertainment Partners. The old name is still sometimes used.

POST-PRODUCTION Editing, sound mixing, CGI - the final elements after filming to put all the material together.

PRE-PRODUCTION The planning, hiring, and scheduling of a production, getting everything ready to shoot.

PROPS Items or objects handled by actors and SA's.

RADIO ETIQUETTE Smooth communication and concise use of the radio.

RAIN MACHINE Almost like a tall shower head used to create rainfall.

RELEASE The artist is no longer in consideration for the role.

REMITTANCE Details on the sum of money that is due to arrive in the artist's bank account.

RING LIGHT An adjustable ring-shaped light on a stand, sometimes with a phone holder.

ROLLING When the camera is recording ready for action.

RUNNER A role that helps out departments with jobs and tasks.

SELF-ASSESSMENT A way to inform HMRC of earnings and expenses within the recent tax year.

SELF-TAPE A requested audition tape recorded at home to send to casting directors for consideration for a role.

SELFIES Quick photos taken by the artist, usually on mobile, and shared.

SET The specific area where filming is taking place. I.e. Garden, balcony, town square, woods, spaceship, lake, stables.

SETTING The time and place the story is taking place. I.e. a fictional village during the "Great Frost" of January 1895.

SOUND SPEED When the sound equipment is recording, ready for the 1st AD to call "action".

SOUNDSTAGE Spacious area that can be designed to suit film, tv, or music recordings.

SPLIT-DAY The entire day is shifted later to allow for both day and night scenes. For example: 14:00 - 02:00.

STANDBY Cameras will be rolling any moment, be ready.

STAND-IN A person substituting in place of an actor to help set up camera, lighting etc.

STANDARD DAY Nine-hour day before overtime starts, including a one-hour lunch break.

STEADICAM A camera harness on the operator used for smooth & steady movements.

STILLS A photographed shot or a still frame from a video.

STUDIO Interior space used for filming, or a collection of sound stages for hire.

TAKE A recorded shot of a scene. Usually done multiple times per camera setup.

TURNAROUND The 11-hour required rest period between wrap and the next day's calltime. Penalty fee payable to artists if this is broken.

UNION An organisation that represents workers within a specific trade or industry.

UNIT BASE The place for department offices, cast trailers, principal costume & makeup to be set up.

USAGE An agreed amount of time a company can use an advert you worked on.

WALK-ON Identifiable and individual from others, but without dialogue.

WILDTRACK Recording audio on a quiet set to capture the ambience, or to collect a mix of vocals from the actors or crowd.

22 COMMON ABBREVIATIONS

Many of these abbreviations will crop up from time to time across the industry or even during this book. Feel free to copy these down or refer back when needed.

AD Assistant Director
AV Availability Request, Or AC meaning Availability Check
BDR Basic Day Rate
BECTU Broadcasting Entertainment Communications and Theatre Union
BG Background
BM Broken Meal
CC Casting Collective
CGI Computer Generated Imagery
COS Costume
CWD Continuous Working Day
DBS Disclosure and Barring Service (formerly CRB)
DFI Don't Follow Instruction/Change Of Mind
EC Early Call
EP Can be Extra People or Entertainment Partners

EXP New abbreviation for Extra People, or Expenses
EXT Exterior/Outdoors
FAA Film Artistes Association
HC Holiday Credit
HETV High End Television
HMRC His Majesty's Revenue and Customs
HMU Hair and Makeup
INT Interior/Inside
LOC Location
MA Meal Allowance
NDA Non-Disclosure Agreement
NIC National Insurance Contributions
OT Overtime
PA Production Assistant
PAYE Pay As You Earn
POC Piece Of Cake
REG Registration
RP Rachel's People
SAG-AFTRA Screen Actors Guild - American Federation of Television and Radio Artists
SD Standard Day
SF Supplementary Fees
SPACT Special Action
TT Talent Talks
TVC Television Commercial
UE Universal Extras
ULEZ Ultra Low Emission Zone
VFX Visual Effects
VO Voiceover

107

P.R.WALTON

ABOUT THE AUTHOR

This book was written by a Supporting Artist who has worked in the industry for more than a decade. Over the years, they have accumulated stories and a wealth of information from their own experiences, allowing them to guide others on a journey of starting their own career or hobby as a film extra. The author lives in Hampshire with regular work across areas of London, Surrey, Sussex, Oxfordshire, and Berkshire.